KW-150

THE ABC'S OF
COCKATIELS

Contents

Photographs: Gerald Allen, 6, 27 (top), 66. Glen Axelrod, 87 (top). Dr. Herbert R. Axelrod, 9 (top), 19, 39 (bottom), 49, 55, 87 (bottom). H. Bielfeld, 83. Elisha W. Burr, 61 (bottom). Michael Gilroy, 91. Manolo Guevara, 61 (top). Ray Hanson, 45 (top), 51 (top), 57 (bottom). B. Kahl, 45 (bottom). J. Maier, 9 (bottom). H. Reinhard, front endpapers, title page, 15, 33, 35, 53, 75. San Diego Zoo, 11, 29, 37 (bottom). Brian Seed, 31. Vincent Serbin, 13, 21, 23, 25, 27 (bottom), 43, 47, back endpapers. Julie Sturman, 37 (top), 57 (top). Vogelpark Walsrode, 17, 41, 63, 67, 71, 79.

Drawings by John R. Quinn unless otherwise credited.

Distributed in the UNITED STATES by T.F.H. Publications, Inc., 211 West Sylvania Avenue, Neptune City, NJ 07753; in CANADA by H & L Pet Supplies Inc., 27 Kingston Crescent, Kitchener, Ontario N2B 2T6; Rolf C. Hagen Ltd., 3225 Sartelon Street, Montreal 382 Quebec; in ENGLAND by T.F.H. Publications Limited, 4 Kier Park, Ascot, Berkshire SL5 7DS; in AUSTRALIA AND THE SOUTH PACIFIC by T.F.H. (Australia) Pty. Ltd., Box 149, Brookvale 2100 N.S.W., Australia; in NEW ZEALAND by Ross Haines & Son, Ltd., 18 Monmouth Street, Grey Lynn, Auckland 2 New Zealand; in SINGAPORE AND MALAYSIA by MPH Distributors (S) Pte., Ltd., 601 Sims Drive, #03/07/21, Singapore 1438; in the PHILIPPINES by Bio-Research, 5 Lippay Street, San Lorenzo Village, Makati Rizal; in SOUTH AFRICA by Multipet Pty. Ltd., 30 Turners Avenue, Durban 4001. Published by T.F.H. Publications, Inc. Manufactured in the United States of America by T.F.H. Publications, Inc.

THE ABC'S OF
COCKATIELS

Wilfried Loeding

Taxonomy

The number of parakeet and parrot fanciers has grown extraordinarily in the last few years and is continuing to increase steadily. Along with the universally known Budgerigar, the Cockatiel *(Nymphicus hollandicus)* is the most frequently kept parakeet among the 600 species and subspecies that make up the family of parrotlike birds (Psittacidae). The Cockatiel can be kept by itself in a cage, learns to repeat a few words, and charms with its amusing personality. It can also help the novice to gain his first experiences of parakeet culture. Cockatiels tend to be fairly willing, hardy breeders; ten to fifteen young in three clutches per year is not unusual. This has contributed to the appearance of various mutations in Cockatiels within the relatively short time of just a few years. Today there are white, yellow, pied, and bordered birds, to list only a few.

At first the new mutations were very expensive, but now, thanks to good breeding practices, they are within everyone's reach. Breeding color varieties of the Cockatiel is an interesting and complex task, equally attractive to the beginner and the experienced aviculturist because of the constant surprises it holds. At regular intervals breeders' clubs organize exhibitions at which prizes are awarded to the best birds of each class.

Juvenile Cockatiel.

In the Wild

"Wild" Cockatiels are slender and measure about 30–32 cm. They are found everywhere in Australia with the exception of the coastal regions. The overall color of the adult cock's plumage is gray. Rump and upper-tail coverts are silver-gray. The under-tail coverts are almost black. Particularly attractive is the yellow head with the long, tapering, lemon-yellow crest. Below the black-colored eyes, each cheek is adorned with a bright red-orange spot. The forward webs of the secondaries and their coverts form a white area. The beak and the fleshy feet are slate-gray.

The hens differ from the cocks mainly by having weaker markings on the head, which makes the head look more grayish in shade, and by the wavy yellow bands on the underside of the tail.

Juveniles are very similar to adult hens, and their sex can only be determined with difficulty. At about six months of age the young cocks get their lemon-yellow head color. The adult coloration, however, is not complete until the birds are about a year old.

In the wild, Cockatiels live in small groups in almost every kind of habitat. They are equally common in dense forests and in savanna-type areas and desertlike spinifex grassland. Cockatiels are nomadic birds; the often vast distances they travel are determined purely by what is available in the way of water and food. In an area which offers favorable living conditions, they breed several times in succession. However, when food becomes less abundant because of the growing number of youngsters, the supernumerary birds are forced to move to other areas where food is less scarce. These movements not infrequently take them near the coast, where they appear in large flocks in localities where they have never been found before. Occasional irruptions

bring them as far as Tasmania and into the eucalyptus forests of southwestern Australia. Usually, however, they return to the Australian interior within a few weeks or months, although a few pairs may well settle down in this new home and breed there. In this way new populations arise; thus the range of these birds has extended more and more toward the coast in the last few decades. This expansion has been further encouraged by the increasingly dry inland climate and large-scale deforestation in the peripheral zones.

Of the parakeets, the Cockatiel is one of the fastest fliers. It flies rapidly, deliberately, and evenly in a straightforward line. When landing on the ground it lets itself drop vertically like a stone and does not reduce speed until just before touchdown. The white on the wing, visible from a long way off when the bird is in flight, presumably serves the purpose of keeping the flock together. During their rapid flight the birds emit a two-syllable call that sounds like *queel-queel*.

Like most other parakeets and parrots, Cockatiels are not particularly ground-dwelling birds. Rather, it is of vital importance for them (as inhabitants of wide, open landscapes) to recognize their enemies in good time. On the ground this is largely made impossible by the vegetation, and the birds' main enemies (smallish to medium-sized birds of prey) have an easy time of it. When feeding on the ground, therefore, Cockatiels take off in a panic at the slightest disturbance, often even without any apparent reason, and return as quickly as possible to their observation posts higher up. Or they endeavor to escape. The birds are particularly wary at watering places. They soar above them for a long time, making sure there are no enemies in the vicinity, before embarking on a plunge into the shallow water. They never land on the shore. Hastily they swallow a few sips of water,

Taxonomy

By wild colored, we mean t
normal gray col

and after no more than a few seconds the whole flock is up and away again. The birds' drinking requirements are not particularly great: as inhabitants of torrid areas they often have to manage without water for fairly long periods.

The birds behave less shyly when perched on the dead branches of trees and shrubs. With their grey color acting as camouflage they can be spotted there only with difficulty. Furthermore, they often adapt their position to that of the twigs and branches. If one stalks them very carefully, one can manage to get to within a few meters of the birds.

Breeding pairs, once they have found each other, stay together the whole year 'round, outside the breeding season living in smallish groups, sometimes in assocation with Budgerigars. Cockatiels generally nest in open holes in the branches of dead trees which afford a good view in all directions. If the nesting tree is big enough, other Cockatiels or cockatoos may also breed there.

In most cases, however, only Budgerigars will be sharing these trees.

When the birds breed depends on the rainy season. In southern Australia the breeding takes place in the spring months (August to December). In the north of their range the birds prefer the end of the rainy season (April to June). By this time the withered plants have recovered and are growing new shoots, flowers, and seeds, so there is plenty of food around for the rearing of young birds. The Cockatiels in central Australia breed whenever conditions happen to be favorable, and again this depends on when the rainy season occurs.

A clutch normally consists of four or five eggs. If food is plentiful, however, there may be as many as six or seven. Like the cockatoos, but unlike other parakeets, both sexes incubate in turn: the cock sits only by day; at night, while the hen sits on the eggs, the cock stands guard just outside the nesting hollow. The chicks

A singly-kept Lutin

hatch after about twenty-one days. The parents then feed and look after the nestlings for four to five weeks. After the young leave the nest cavity, the parents continue to feed them for a few more weeks until they are fully independent.

The diet of Cockatiels includes the seeds of nearly all the different grasses and herbs, either half-ripe or ripe. The birds have also been seen on flowering eucalyptus trees, where they appeared to be feeding on nectar or insects. In areas where wheat is grown on a major scale, Cockatiels are among the most common birds (they are by no means considered harmful to the crop, however.) Flocks of up to 200 birds have been observed in such instances.

In the past, farmers poisoned some of the watering places or put out poisoned grain. Although this was not always aimed at Cockatiels, many of them died as a result; and while such measures now belong to the past, Cockatiels are either not protected at all in the various Australian states or they are protected only at certain times of the year. The sheer size of Australia is an additional obstacle to effective regulation.

Another source of danger to Cockatiels is motorists. The birds fly onto the road to pick up bits of gravel which they need for their digestion. Usually, however, they manage to take off before an approaching car gets too close.

The Cockatiel was discovered by deported British convicts living in the penal colonies of Australia, which was then British. The first scientific description was provided toward the end of the eighteenth century by the scientist Gmelin in his work *Systema naturae*. Because of its resemblance to the cockatoos, Gmelin called the bird the "wedge-tailed cockatoo" or "cockatoo parakeet" *(Psittacus novae-hollandiae)*. Detailed reports on this parakeet in the wild were supplied by Gould around 1840.

In 1845, or probably before

Two of many Cockatiel color varieties—a Pearled and a Lutino.

that, the first Cockatiels came to Europe, first to England, where they were brought by seamen. Unfortunately, most of these birds could not tolerate the damp English climate and did not survive for long. Thanks to the growing general interest in ornithology and new imports on a large scale, more and more Cockatiels continued to reach Europe, until the Australian government decided on an export embargo. Today the demand for Cockatiels can be met entirely through birds bred in captivity.

It is likely that the first successful attempts at breeding the Cockatiel in captivity were made around 1850 in Hamburg and Frankfurt, although earlier attempts, in 1846, were reported from the *Jardin des plantes* in Paris (whether these succeeded is not known). In 1858 Leuckfeld published the first detailed accounts of keeping and breeding Cockatiels. From then on the species became well known and was given a place in many zoological gardens and private aviaries.

The table below supplies a survey of when the Cockatiel was first bred in various countries:

Ca. 1850	First captive breeding in the world in Hamburg and Frankfurt
1863	First bred in Britain (London Zoo)
Ca. 1865	First bred in Holland
1881	First bred in Switzerland
Ca. 1890	First bred in Belgium
Ca. 1900	First bred in India
Ca. 1910	First bred in the U.S.A.
Ca. 1920	First bred in Japan

Its Taxonomic Position

The taxonomic position of the Cockatiel continues to be highly controversial even today. Older authors such as Gould (1865) and Russ (1881)

A Pearl Pied Cockatiel.

place it among the cockatoos. More recent authors—Neunzig (1921), Peters (1937), Berndt and Meise (1962), and Boetticher (1964)—locate it with the broad-tailed parakeets (rosellas *et al.*). Neither theory is entirely sound when one compares the appearance and behavior of Cockatiels, cockatoos, and broad-tailed parakeets.

The crest, color patches on the cheeks, feathered cere, and the fact that the cock helps to incubate the eggs all point toward relationship with cockatoos. Conversely, the parakeetlike shape and the long tail indicate that the Cockatiel belongs with the broad-tailed parakeets. Unlike them, however, Cockatiels make scooping movements when drinking and lay the head back in order to swallow the water. Also, their courtship, threat, and reproductive behaviors have more in common with those of the cockatoos. A parallel evolution of the broad-tailed parakeets and the cockatoos seems very vague.

Too many factors suggest that the Cockatiel is related to the cockatoos. However, attempts to cross Cockatiels and cockatoos have so far never been productive. Hybridization with broad-tailed parakeets is said to have occurred, especially with the Red-rumped and Blue-winged Parrots. But it is doubtful that this information is based on fact, as there have been no reports of any repetitions of these crosses.

Personally, I—like Forshaw (1973)—believe that the Cockatiel occupies a special position and cannot be classed as belonging to the subfamily of cockatoos (Cacatuninae). Rather, the Cockatiel represents a subfamily of its own (Nymphicinae), which together with the Cacatuinae forms the family of cockatoos (Cacatuidae).

Selecting

Lutinos are among the more commonly available Cockatiels.

Selecting a Cockatiel

Anyone wishing to keep and train a single pet Cockatiel should purchase it at a pet shop or from a breeder. Wherever possible, select a bird which is still at the nestling stage, with the eyes still entirely black, without light iridial rings. Since immature birds do not yet have the full, characteristic plumage, sexing is difficult if not impossible at this stage. Where wild-colored (gray) Cockatiels are concerned, young cocks can sometimes already be identified by more conspicuously yellow feathers in the head region. With regard to keeping, however, it does not really matter which sex the bird is. What is important is that one choose a pet from a healthy stock. The plumage should be smooth and close-lying. The bird must not keep its head tucked into its feathers, as this indicates poor health or the presence of disease. A bird with some abnormality of the feet or claws should not be

selected either. If one has a choice, a candidate which is a little bit on the shy side is preferable to one that is too bold.

Anyone wishing to acquire Cockatiels for breeding purposes should get in touch with a fancier or a breeder. Fc breeding one should select birds with full adult plumage and make sure that the members of a pair are not closely related. The newly purchased birds should not be allowed immediate contact wit any existing stock but kept under close observation in an isolation cage for one to two weeks to check whether they are indeed in good health and to worm them if necessary. Only then can the newcomers be permitted to share an aviar with other birds. Ideally the move should take place in the morning so that the birds have until dusk to get used to their new surroundings. Drastic changes in temperature must be avoided when transferring the pair. Food should at first be the mixture the birds

On this horizontally w[...]
cage, the foor swings dowr
allow the Cockatiel a place
climb in and [...]

received in their previous home; then they can gradually be accustomed to a new diet.

Accommodation

Depending on whether we wish to keep a single bird as a pet or several birds for breeding, we have to provide suitable accommodations. A tame Cockatiel can be housed in a spacious cage for large parakeets or in an indoor flight. If the bird will be kept in a colony with others or if breeding is the goal, then a spacious aviary is essential.

The Cage

There are many different cages on the market, but only a few models are truly functional and really meet the needs of their prospective occupants. The ideal cage for a Cockatiel is an all-metal one, since it is easy to clean and is able to withstand the parakeet's chewing urge. The cage should not be smaller than about 60 x 40 x 30 cm. A bigger cage is, however, much to be preferred, as it ensures that the bird can move about sufficiently without knocking against the metal wire with its tail or wings every time it turns around. Further, it is important that the wires run horizontally on at least two sides so that the Cockatiel is able to satisfy its climbing needs. The bottom of the cage should be equipped with a deep plastic tray with one or more drawers. The plastic tray ensures that the scattering of food and sand is reduced to a minimum, and the drawers make it easier to clean the bottom of the cage. The dowel perches that come with most cages should be removed straightaway and replaced with natural branches (e.g., from willow, hazel-nut, or fruit trees) on which the Cockatiel can chew to its heart's content. From time to time these are replaced with fresh ones. I prefer natural branches not only because they are rich in

Since Cockatiels feel secure on high perches, curtain rods are favored resting spots.

vitamins under the bark but also because they never have any one diameter—this exercises the Cockatiel's leg and foot muscles in a natural way. The cage should not be fitted with too many perches and swings because they will restrict the already limited freedom of movement still further.

Another particularly important point is the location of the cage. Parakeets need to be in a light, draft-free spot. They must not, however, be exposed to bright sunlight for any length of time. Sudden fluctuations in temperature in the room where the cage stands should also be avoided. Cockatiels can rapidly lose their tameness if housed unsuitably or if their cage has been placed in the wrong spot. Ideally, one should choose a room which is frequented by the keeper or other people, since Cockatiels are sociable birds. As they are also easily frightened, however, they must be given the opportunity to see when people are approaching.

Food should be placed on the bottom of the cage in heavy earthenware or porcelain containers, which do not tip over as easily as plastic ones. To obviate, as far as possible, contamination from the bird's own droppings, it is important not to place the food vessels directly under the perches.

It goes without saying that a Cockatiel which spends most of its life inside a cage must have ample opportunity for exercise. The bird should, therefore, be allowed to fly about in the room at regular intervals—under supervision, however, since Cockatiels can do considerable damage with their powerful beaks.

The Indoor Aviary

The biggest cage can never be big enough; so with Cockatiels too it is best to accommodate them in a spacious room or indoor aviary. Depending on what an indoor aviary is to be used for (e.g., for breeding or for

So long as Cockatiels are housed in large, roomy cages, they won't need freedom outside their cages

accommodation with other birds), it can be set up in the attic, basement, or shed. Here too the same requirements apply as for cages: brightness, minimal fluctuations in temperature, and no drafts. The handy person can easily make his own indoor aviary, using wire mesh and wooden boards. In the case of indoor aviaries one generally dispenses with cage floor and drawers and uses the natural floor instead, to which one gains access for cleaning through a low door. The food vessels should be placed on a shelf fitted half-way up the wall.

The Outdoor Aviary

The ideal accommodation for Cockatiels is an outdoor aviary with a shelter room. Needless to say, one requires a garden and perhaps a building permit. In addition, it is advisable to get the neighbors' permission, since Cockatiels, like all parrots and parakeets, can be very noisy, particularly when

kept in larger numbers. The aviary may consist of one compartment or more; none should be smaller than about 2.50 x 1.00 x 2.00 m. (outdoor flight) and 1.00 x 1.00 x 2.00 m. (shelter room). The construction, of course, depends on where one lives and how much money one is able or willing to spend. To avoid unsuitable planning and subsequent alterations, it is advisable to talk to experienced breeders before beginning to build.

A concrete foundation about 80 cm. in depth underneath the whole structure prevents rats and mice from getting in. For the shelter, one uses bricks, wood, or manufactured sheetings. The outdoor flight is constructed of wooden framing and fine wire mesh. The mesh should be as small as possible to prevent unwelcome guests—such as small mice or perhaps even a weasel—from squeezing through. The shelter must be bright and well-insulated. Heating is not essential for Cockatiels, as they

When not feeding, Cockatiels are inclined to perch on bare branches (*above*). Their diet consists chiefly of seeds (*below*).

can survive temperatures of −15 C. unharmed if they are not exposed to a draft.

Provision should be made for a walk-way from which each shelter room can be reached. The food is most conveniently offered on a feeding shelf above the low entrance door. A hole ensures that the birds are able, at all times, to move from the shelter room into the outdoor flight. The outdoor flights must be designed in such a way that each one of them is readily accessible. One either has a wire-enclosed walk-way going along the front of all the outdoor flights—which prevents the birds from escaping through the open aviary door—or, alternatively, one connects all the aviary compartments to one another by means of low doors. In this latter arrangement a small vestibule outside the first door will suffice. The floor of the shelter room should be covered with gravel; in the outdoor flight the natural ground can be kept uncovered. There is not much

point in planting the aviary, as the Cockatiels would chew all the vegetation to bits within just a few hours. A better method is to rake seeds and food remnants into the ground from time to time—these will quickly germinate and provide a dietary supplement which is rich in vitamins. The perches should be fitted along the further sides of the flight so that they do not take up valuable flying space (which is limited enough as it is). A few fresh branches are stuck into the ground for the birds to chew and must be replaced when necessary. Drinking water is supplied in the outdoor flight in a big, shallow dish. Low bushes or shrubs should be planted outside the aviary to give the birds a feeling of security in their new home.

Feeding

Cockatiels are considered very undemanding with regard to their food. Their basic, or

Normal cock

main, diet consists of various seeds. If a single bird is kept, it is advisable to feed it commercial seed mixtures made up of sunflower seeds, hemp, oats, wheat, peanuts, and millet. If there are several birds, however, it strikes me as better to offer each food separately in a little earthenware or porcelain dish. This feeding method has the advantage of ensuring that the different types of seeds are always available in sufficient quantities and that less food is scattered about and wasted. It is a fact that while some birds prefer white sunflower seeds, others choose striped ones. Every bird has its favorite seeds, and what these are may vary with the season and again during the breeding season or the molt. If one uses ready-mixed seeds, those that are not currently favored will simply be thrown out of the container and scattered carelessly. If there is not enough room on the feeding-shelf, smallish seeds such as millet (Budgerigar seed-mixture),

canary seed, niger, and some linseed may be served mixed. Sunflower seeds, however, which are the main food, must always be offered in a separate dish. From time to time a few peanut kernels may be sprinkled over them. Hemp must be used with care because it has a high oil content. If given more or less exclusively, the birds tend to become fat. But this does not mean it should not be available in small quantities at all times, particularly before and during the breeding season and in the cold winter months. Cereals, such as oats (hulled and unhulled) and wheat, should always be available, even if they are often turned down. A special favorite is spray millet; it should be hung up in generous amounts.

Besides the seeds, various kinds of fruit and greenfood should also be provided. Depending on the season, the birds can be given apples, pears, carrots, and various types of berries (such as rosehips, rowan, and

Feeding

A pair of Cinn
Cocka

hawthorne.) As greenfood and sources of half-ripe seeds (both rich in vitamins), chickweed (above all), dandelion (especially its blossoms), carrot leaves, common groundsel, lettuce, and spinach are suitable. Unripened sunflower seeds from one's own garden can be offered too; in fact, the birds are particularly partial to these.

During the breeding season and in the winter when greenfood has become scarcer, we add sprouted seeds to the birds' fare. Particularly suitable in this respect are oats and sunflower seeds. The required quantity of food is soaked in water in a strainer for twenty-four hours, rinsed well, and left to stand for another twenty-four hours, without water, until it is just beginning to sprout. This type of sprouted food is a great favorite with all parakeets. It is important, however, that the seed has been rinsed thoroughly and that we do not offer too much of it. If it

ferments, as easily happens, can be harmful to the birds.

During the rearing period supplement the birds' diet w white rolls or wheat bread soaked in water and mixed with egg yolk and a commercial rearing food. Various brands of prepared rearing foods are available, some of which can only be given dry, some only moistened, while others may be used either way. These products also contain vitami and trace elements; therefore they must not be stored for long periods, as some ingredients become ineffectiv

Trace elements and vitami. also become available to Cockatiels when they chew o branches and twigs. Particularly under the bark a in the buds of flowers and leaves are there substances which are vital for the birds' growth and maintenance of their health. For this reason plentiful supply of branches from willow, hazel-nut, or fr trees is absolutely essential.

Feeding

Often one can see Cockatiels picking up grains of sand from the floor. They require these both for their digestion and for the important minerals they contain. Calcium may be provided to them in the form of cuttlebone, calcium and mineral blocks, and the grated shells of mussels and eggs.

Vitamin preparations, of which many are available on the market, should be treated with caution and administered, if at all, only in the cold winter months. If the birds get more vitamins than they need, the disadvantages will outweigh the advantages and one possible side-effect could be a premature molt. Overdosages can sometimes be very dangerous. It is advisable, therefore,—except in certain exceptional situations such as illness, etc.—to avoid the artificial administration of vitamins and instead to make the diet as varied and nutritious as possible in respect to seeds, fruit, greenfood, minerals, and trace elements. The birds instinctively select the vitamins they need in the right quantities.

Cockatiels should be given only water to drink—unchlorinated, if possible—although they may b offered a little chamomile tea when ill. As they originate in the dry areas of Australia, the will come to no harm if left without water for a couple of days. Often they make do with small drops of water adhering to the greenfood. Without food, on the other hand, they could not survive even for a day, since the metabolism of birds is very much faster than that of mammals, which mean their fat reserves can rapidly become depleted.

In conclusion, I would like particularly to dissuade the keepers of single birds from treating their pets to human fare in the form of left-overs and stimulants such as coffee or alcohol. Many "fanciers" who foster such addictions fin them especially endearing and do not stop to think how muc harm they do to their pets. Generally, such humanized

One bird preens the other' crest feathers

creatures meet an early, painful death from liver damage or disorders of other vital organs.

Breeding

At some point or other almost everyone who owns a garden aviary or a large indoor flight will feel the wish to propagate his pets. Successful breeding undoubtedly is the highest goal a bird fancier can set himself. I must point out here, however, that [in Germany] under the psittacosis regulations anyone wanting to breed parakeets or parrots must first obtain a license. The license granting permission for breeding and trading is issued by the veterinary department of the local authorities. To qualify for it, applicants must pass a short test covering fundamentals about diseases, notably psittacosis, and general knowledge on breeding and keeping. Also, the applicant is required to keep a written record of buying, breeding, selling, and mortality of his birds. Young birds must be banded in accordance with the regulations. Open bands are available from the *Zentralverband Zoologischer Fachgeschafte* in Frankfurt am Main. Closed bands are supplied to members of the *Geschaftsstelle der Austauschzentrale der Vogelliebhaber und -zuchter* ("*AZ*," for short), the German association of bird fanciers and breeders.

The fact that the Cockatiel is easy to breed makes it an ideal first species for anyone who has never propagated large parakeets before and would like to gain experience. The first breeding experiments are best carried out with gray (i.e., wild-colored) Cockatiels. Here the sexes are much easier to differentiate than they are where the many mutations are concerned. The breeding birds should not be less than twelve months old. In this way one avoids having to cope with undesirable side-effects such as unfertilized clutches and incomplete incubation,

Breeding

Coition will be successful if stable perches are provided *(above)*. Lutino nestling *(below)*.

although some younger Cockatiels do manage to breed successfully and to rear their chicks. Breeding Cockatiels should be given a separate compartment in the aviary. Communal breeding (with Budgerigars, exotics, or other pairs of Cockatiels) should only be attempted with experienced breeding pairs in extra-spacious aviaries. Where a shelter room is available, it should be equipped with one or two nest boxes, each with a base of 25 x 25 cm., a height of 30 cm., and an entrance hole measuring about 8-10 cm. in diameter. If there is no shelter room or it is too small, the boxes should be hung inside the roofed-over part of the outdoor flight.

Cockatiels are not particular about the shape and appearance of their nest boxes. There is no reason why one should not make the box oneself, using chipboard or wood. The use of brand-new materials (still smelling of glue, etc.) should be avoided, however. Like the vast majority of

parakeets and parrots, Cockatiels do not build a proper nest but merely deposit their eggs on the floor of the nest box. For this reason the box should be lined with a layer 3-4 cm. thick of damp peat fibers mixed with a small quantity of wood shavings. In the center of this one makes a (roughly) fist-sized depression into which the female will later lay her eggs. The depression is intended to prevent the eggs from rolling around. Some breeders dispense with the layer of peat fibers and place a wooden board with a suitable hollow on the floor of the nest box. Cockatiels are not all that choosy and, rather like Budgerigars, will accept what we offer them. Personally, I prefer the first method, however. On a bare, dry board the eggs are much more likely to dry out.

The nest boxes are hung up in the spring: either March or April, depending on the weather (earlier, if one likes, provided shelter rooms are available). The pair will soon

36

Breeding

become interested in the nest boxes and embark on their courtship, which is beautiful to watch. The cock displays his yellow crest and walks round the hen with quick, small steps, his wings raised and slightly spread out. Often, on these occasions, he keeps his head lowered and his tail erect and spread out like a fan, whistling loudly at the same time. Unlike other parakeets, the feeding ritual is absent. Instead, one can observe a wheeling courtship flight. This, if the hen is willing, is followed by copulation, during which the cock makes low, soothing noises.

After about ten to fourteen days the hen lays one egg every other day until the clutch is complete; it will consist of four to six eggs. Clutches of up to nine eggs are not unusual, however. Incubation begins when the second egg has been laid and continues for about eighteen to nineteen days. Unlike other male parakeets, the male Cockatiel helps the hen with the incubating. The cock sits on the eggs during the day, and the hen takes over at night. During the night, though sometimes in the daytime too, the two partners stay inside the nest box.

At the time of hatching, the chicks are covered in pale yellow down, apart from a bald patch at the back of the head. After about eighteen days the spots on the cheeks begin to appear, and after about four weeks the plumage is fully developed. The eyes open at the age of five to ten days. At this point the young must be closed-banded.

When opening the nest box to inspect, one can hear a loud hissing to croaking emitted by the young, which will continue for some time after the flap has been closed. Later, some of the young may even attack the intruding hand with their beaks.

The beak is flesh-colored at first, then turns brownish, and eventually, at the age of three months, it grows dark. When the young are four to five

A Lutino with characteristi‹ red eyes

weeks old, they leave the nest box. At this stage they are usually very wild, and their first attempts at flying look clumsy and unskilled. For this reason it is advisable to stick a few branches through the aviary wire, just before the young are due to fledge, to mark the obstacle and prevent unnecessary injuries. This wildness usually disappears after a few days. It is lovely to watch the parent birds feed their chicks. A mere fourteen days after fledging the young start to feed independently, although they still ask their parents for food as well. When begging to be fed, they crouch on the perch and shriek loudly. This serves as a trigger for the parents to regurgitate their food and pass it to the young.

Good breeding pairs raise two or three broods per year, which often results in the considerable total of as many as fifteen young. After each brood the nest box, heavily fouled by the young, should be cleaned thoroughly. Only in this way can one prevent pests.

After the third brood, if not before, the nest box is removed and disinfected. (No breeder should permit his birds to have more than three broods.) It is then put away, ready for use the following year.

At the latest, the young should be separated from their parents when the next brood is expected to hatch. Otherwise, they will disturb the rearing of the new chicks. After eight or nine months the young show the full adult colors, and the young cocks start their first courtship displays.

Cockatiels have on many occasions been successfully used as foster parents to raise young birds of other species, e.g., various broadtails, such as the Eastern and Western Rosellas. On the other hand, Budgerigars have been known to incubate and rear Cockatiels.

Occasionally it can happen that the parents suddenly stop feeding their young. Where this is the case, the aviculturist is forced to hand-rear the youngsters. This demands a

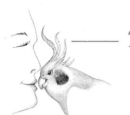

Repetition and review are t
keys to teaching a tar
Cockatiel how to ta

great deal of time and patience. The best way to go about it is to get a syringe. A piece of rubber tubing is pushed over the tip, to avoid injuring the beak and throat of the chicks when feeding them. The young birds should be given a soft, lukewarm pulp consisting of baby food, grated carrots, chopped greenfood, etc. every two to three hours. This food should be put into their beaks drop by drop. The young Cockatiels swallow quickly and without any problem. When they have grown bigger, one can use a spoon to feed them. Such hand-reared young birds become very tame, of course, and form a close relationship with their keeper. They make excellent cage birds. Though it is laborious to rear the birds, it is well worth the trouble.

The Tame Cockatiel

As already mentioned, the Cockatiel—along with the Budgerigar—is one of the most frequently kept psittacine

birds. For many families wanting a single bird the Cockatiel is a definite favorite. That the species became so well established in German households is due mainly to its pretty, elegant appearance (it bears a resemblance to a cockatoo) and its keen ability to learn. Over and above that, it is invariably very reasonable to buy, compared with other parrot and parakeet species. Many people without the slightest intention of ever keeping a bird in the house have been charmed into the hobby by a tame Cockatiel: the birds tend to be creatures full of life and fun, which are also able to sing melodiously and to mimic a few words of human speech. Particularly decorative in the home are the colorful varieties such as pearled, bordered, and pied birds or the pure white Cockatiels which look like miniature cockatoos. The important points to remember in regard to purchase, accommodation, and nutrition have already been outlined. But what exactly can

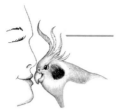

Taming

This young Cockatie[l] illustrates the tameness tha[t] results from hand-rearing *(above)*. Wild-colored (gray[)] Cockatiel cock *(below)*

we do to ensure that our newly acquired pet becomes tame and learns to imitate a few words or simple tunes?

Any bird one wants to talk must be absolutely tame. The young bird, still foolishly shy, must first grow to trust its keeper and its surroundings. A newly acquired Cockatiel must, therefore, be kept by itself, i.e., neither with other Cockatiels nor with birds of other species. Where the cage is put should be decided beforehand, as the Cockatiel will grow even more agitated if we keep moving its cage about. Also, the cage should already be fully equipped (with food, sand, perches, etc.) and ready for use by the time the Cockatiel arrives. It is advisable to offer special tidbits (such as millet sprays) in the cage on the first day. Only when all is ready can we risk releasing the newcomer from its dark transport case into its new home. This must be done carefully and without other birds being around. No bird will take kindly to being

grabbed and pushed into a new "prison" immediately after its arrival. When the young Cockatiel has climbed into the cage, we have to give it a chance to get to know its new surroundings. At this stage it is best to leave it alone—a watching pair of eyes will only increase its agitation. During the first few nights the room containing the cage should never be left completely without illumination. A dim night light will help the Cockatiel find its way about in the unfamiliar surroundings, should it get startled and fall off its perch.

In the early stages, whenever one has to go near the bird, one should proceed as carefully and quietly as possible. The still shy bird should be calmed down by talking to it until it stops fluttering about wildly in the cage. Flight outside the cage must never be permitted during the first few days. Until the bird has learned to regard the cage as its own territory, where it receives food and can have privacy and rest, it is

44

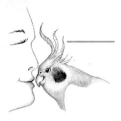

Hand-taming benefits a single Cockatiel.

unlikely to return to the cage voluntarily. The keeper would then be obliged to go after and catch it, which would cause the Cockatiel further anxiety. If the keeper talks to the bird often and gently, the bird will eventually remain on its perch when he approaches. In fact, the bird will await his approach with interest, wondering what will happen next, and may even respond to the keeper's calm voice with a shy whistling noise.

Once this stage has been reached, we have made considerable progress and the first hurdle has been cleared. Now we can start, slowly and cautiously, to offer tidbits (such as millet sprays) through the cage bars. If the bird accepts them, one can try offering them through the open cage door. It is important, however, that the keeper remains absolutely calm while doing this and moves as little as possible, to avoid startling the bird. If the Cockatiel panics nonetheless, one has to start all over again,

continuing until it has become tame enough to eat trustingly out of one's hand. When the bird has been used to the keeper's hand for a while, one proceeds to gently stroke the bird's breast with the index finger. After several such caresses one increases the pressure slightly (provided the bird shows no sign of fear), thus forcing the little Cockatiel to climb onto the outstretched finger. If it seeks to avoid it, one goes on trying by slowly following it with the finger and talking gently. Soon the parakeet will lose its fear and climb onto the hand quite voluntarily in order to get at the desired tidbit. If it pecks at the hand or chews on it (which can sometimes be very painful), one must on no account withdraw one's hand quickly, as this would frighten the bird. The secret of taming and handling Cockatiels consists of patience and quietness. Cockatiels are by nature easily startled and agitated. The slightest disturbance makes them take

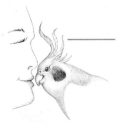

This young Cockatiel is already strong enough to inflict a painful bite

off and fly away.

Eventually, when the little Cockatiel has lost all fear of the human hand and gets on it inside the cage without prompting, one can try—slowly—to take the bird out of the cage while it is sitting on one's hand. Soon it will climb up the keeper like a tree, endeavoring to get to the highest point, i.e., a shoulder or even the head. It will also like to fly around the room a few times. Before allowing it to do this, however, one has to make sure all windows and doors are closed. Be sure the Cockatiel can clearly recognize the window panes (e.g., by drawn curtains); otherwise it may accidentally fly into them and sustain an injury or fly off through the open window. An escaped Cockatiel is difficult to recapture since it quickly becomes disorientated and gets hopelessly lost. Due to lack of food and unfamiliar dangers such as cars or birds of prey, it is often condemned to an early death.

When the Cockatiel has finished with its first flight around the room, we are usually confronted with the problem of how to lure it back inside the cage. Usually it returns voluntarily only if driven by hunger or thirst. Where these are absent, it prefers to find itself a high perch from which it can survey the room. One should first try the welcoming extended forefinger in the usual way. If it climbs on, one tries to return it to the cage, moving very slowly, and shuts the door behind it. If this attempt fails and the bird escapes to a high perch such as the popular curtain rail or a tall cupboard, one must not panic. One should never pursue the bird in order to drive it back to the cage, nor should one reach for it with one's hand. The bird would then become frightened of hand and keeper and never return to him voluntarily. It is best to postpone recapturing the bird until the evening. Note where the bird is

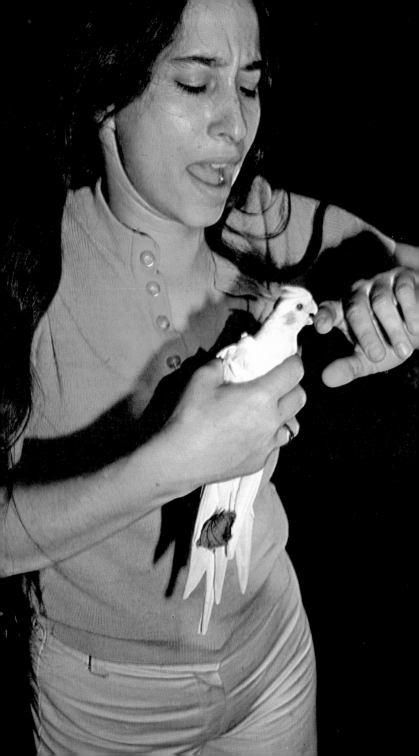

Taming

A few days' supply of sm
seeds can be offered i
dispenser *(above)*. Diet
important for good hea
(belo

perched, switch off the light, grab the bird with the help of a cloth, and put it back into the cage. In the dark it cannot identify the grabbing hand and therefore cannot come to associate it with danger. In order that the bird learns to return to the cage on its own initiative, it should never be fed outside the cage. If it receives food only inside its cage, food and cage will soon become synonymous, and it will then accept the cage as his home. Soon it will learn to fly back into the cage voluntarily when it feels hungry or wants to have peace and quiet.

Cockatiels kept in cages should be given the opportunity to fly outside the cage once a day so that they can satisfy their natural desire for movement and do not grow too fat. It is important, however, that this daily flight always take place under supervision. Otherwise the Cockatiel will use its strong beak to investigate all sorts of things, to the detriment of furniture and fittings.

It is in the nature of almost all parrotlike birds to live in close association with one or more of their own kind. For this reason a solitary Cockatiel, missing the company of its own kind, readily attaches itself to a human being and gives him all its affection. It likes the presence of human beings and hates being by itself. Because of this, Cockatiels that have been left alone for a long time can become noisy vandals. They can make a lot of noise and become very destructive. Conversely, a Cockatiel which gets enough attention rewards its keeper with an extraordinary sweetness of nature.

Cockatiels learn easily and are able to mimic words or tunes. Some even learn simple tricks, since these birds have a very strongly developed urge to play. However, a lot of patience is required on the part of the keeper if the bird is to learn simple tricks. Furthermore, the bird has to have a certain amount of

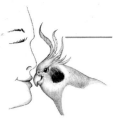

By purchasing a matu[re]
Cockatiel, there can be [no]
question as to its se[x]

talent. In order to learn to talk or mimic tunes the Cockatiel must be very tame and trusting. Time and time again one has to whistle the tune or say the words one wants it to learn. Needless to say, one cannot start off with whole sentences or songs but only with single words or parts of a melody. Cockatiels are at their most attentive in the evenings. Often it will take a considerable time before the Cockatiel—presumably when alone and longing for its "mate" (in this case, the keeper)—repeats the word or tune it has heard so often, repeating it indistinctly at first but more clearly later on.

The "speech" of Cockatiels is, of course, not nearly as distinct as, for example, that of an African Grey Parrot. Rather, it resembles that of a Budgerigar, although one is still perfectly able to make it out. The easiest words for a Cockatiel to say are words with many vowels such as *coco*, *bubi*, etc. Once the bird has learned one word, it will soon be able to pick up others. One must remember, however, to review frequently what has been learned already; otherwise the bird will forget its earlier vocabulary. Simple tunes come more easily to a Cockatiel than do words, as it is in the nature of this species to mimic all sorts of whistling and piping sounds with enthusiasm. Cockatiels kept in outdoor aviaries are sometimes heard to perform convincing imitations of a Blackbird's call.

Many weeks or months may pass before one succeeds in teaching one's Cockatiel to mimic speech (one cannot really call it talking since the bird does not understand the meaning of the words, although there may be times when it accidentally says the right word at the right time). Some Cockatiels are quicker learners than others. The keeper must never lose heart and give up, however, for whether the Cockatiel learns to talk and when it begins to do so depend on how often one has time for teaching. Even a

Pearl cock and h[...]

very slow learner may catch on eventually. However, talking or not, a tame Cockatiel never fails to give pleasure to its keeper with its affection and tenderness.

Keeping a tame Cockatiel in one's home has its drawbacks, of course. And by this I mean the considerable extra work that it involves for the housewife (usually). At least twice a week the bottom of the cage (which in modern cages consists of a plastic tray) must be cleaned and sprinkled with fresh bird sand. In addition, the whole cage, including perches, must be washed down with water at fairly frequent intervals and perhaps disinfected as well. Furthermore, the floor of the room and any furniture in the vicinity of the cage get dirty much more quickly than they would normally, due to food remnants and husks and small feathers thrown out of the cage, particularly during the molting periods.

On no account should the Cockatiel's cage be jammed full of toys of every description, depriving the bird of what little room for exercise we have been able to provide. It is far better to give it a separate small playground in the form of a climbing tree next to or on top of the cage. The climbing tree consists of freshly cut twigs from fruit or willow trees and can be replaced without difficulty when necessary.

Apart from the points mentioned, a tame Cockatiel makes no special demands on his keeper, except perhaps in one respect: Some Cockatiels love being sprayed now and then with a plant sprayer filled with tepid water, until they are wet through. After the shower the bird preens itself, and the plumage ends up looking shiny and new. Alternatively, one could put a bathing dish at the bird's disposal. Some Cockatiels make use of these with great regularity and enthusiasm.

There is no need to cover the Cockatiel's cage with a cloth at night. In my opinion,

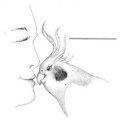

Perching and preening a
usual activities *(above)*. Th
Cockatiel *(below)* is about
engage in free fligh

it is preferable to let the bird
see and take part in what goes
on in the room until the lights
are switched off at bedtime.
This also enables it to enjoy
the first rays of sunshine in the
morning and to witness the
gradual return of daylight. Or
would you, as the keeper, want
to get up at three in the
morning in the summer
months just to take the cover
off the cage? If the bird is very
tired, it catches up on lost
sleep in the daytime.

The Cockatiel Kept with Other Birds

The Cockatiel is one of the
really peaceable parakeets. It
loves company and, provided
the aviary is big enough, can
be kept and bred perfectly well
in a colony with Budgerigars.
Despite their size, Cockatiels
are harmless and, if danger
threatens, defend no more than
a small area around their nest
box. In a large aviary
Cockatiels may also be kept
together with the equally

peace-loving Bourke's Parakeet
or other species of grass
parakeet (Elegant, Scarlet-
chested, or Turquoise
Parakeets). It is important,
however, to watch this
community very carefully so
that any bird seen to disturb
the peace can be removed
immediately. With colony
breeding, it is advisable to
provide each breeding pair
with at least two nest boxes so
that squabbles over breeding
sites are avoided. Colony
breeding of several pairs of
Cockatiels can be successful
too. Year after year I have
managed to raise three broods
(in an aviary of 3 x 5 m., with
a shelter room) from a pair of
wild-colored and a pair of
white Cockatiels. It is
important, however, in this
situation to select only
breeding pairs of proven
reliability, which are firmly
attached to one another.
    It is also possible to keep a
colorful assortment of
Cockatiels and other exotic
birds in the same aviary. In
such cases however, it is

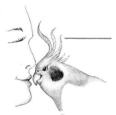

An illustration by A.F. Lyd which appeared in W Greene's *Parrots in Captiv*

important that the small exotic birds such as grassfinches, siskins, and weavers are allowed to get used to the (comparatively speaking) enormous Cockatiels very gradually. If the exotic birds are to breed in the communal aviary, it is advisable to protect their nest baskets and boxes with wide-meshed wire that allows the little birds to slip through while keeping out the Cockatiels. Otherwise, the curious Cockatiels may investigate the nests and destroy them in the process.

Where breeding is not a priority, the following selection would be very colorful and attractive to look at: one pair of Cockatiels, one pair of Bourke's Parakeets, one or two pairs of Budgerigars, several pairs of small exotic birds such as Zebra Finches, Gouldian Finches, ornamental doves, etc., and for the bottom a pair of dwarf quail. A collection of this kind requires an aviary of about 3 x 5 x 2 m. and a heated shelter room for the winter months.

With all community aviaries, it is important to avoid overstocking. All the inhabitants must have enough room to fly, and they all need roosting places appropriate to their kind.

Cockatiels at Liberty

Liberty, in this context, is taken to mean not the liberty of a tame Cockatiel in the living room but truly free flight out of doors, as a result of which Cockatiels become established in our latitudes.

In recent years many breeders and fanciers have carried out such liberty experiments with Budgerigars, Monk and Alexandrine Parakeets, Peach-faced Lovebirds, Zebra Finches, Java Sparrows, and Cockatiels. Since Cockatiels are able to survive the winter out of doors if necessary, one simply opened the aviary doors for a while (as soon as the offspring had hatched) and allowed the birds to fly in and out as they

Medicines can be given
means of a syringe *(abou
After surgery, a single sut
may be used to close
incision *(belo

pleased. During these
experiments food and water
were provided both inside and
outside the aviary. While it is
very nice to watch exotic birds
flying free in our latitudes,
nearly all experiments carried
out so far have failed (one of
the exceptions being those with
Monk and Alexandrine
Parakeets in the Berlin and
Cologne Zoos).
Cockatiels in particular are
little inclined to settle in one
place. They travel vast
distances, often do not find
their way back, and cause
considerable damage to the
fruit trees in the neighborhood.
In addition, many of them fall
prey to such natural enemies as
hawks and domestic cats.
Personally, I do not approve of
such experiments. They give a
criminally false picture of our
native bird life, and most of
the birds involved in them are
doomed to an early and painful
death.

Diseases

Cockatiels are extraordinarily
hardy birds, very resistant to
diseases. Nevertheless, it can
happen that they contract a
minor cold or enteritis. A sick
Cockatiel is easy enough to
identify: it sits about with
fluffed-out feathers and hides
its head in its plumage. If the
bird looks apathetic, suffers
from a nasal discharge or
inflamed eyes, or shivers
visibly, then we know all is not
well. Droppings too can
indicate ill health: if they are
runny instead of solid or are
suddenly of a different color. I
hasten to add, however, that
liquid feces are not invariably a
sign of disease. Sometimes they
merely result from an excessive
intake of greens or soft food.

Undoubtedly the most
dreaded disease, with all
parrots and parakeets, is
psittacosis ("parrot
disease")—or, more correctly,
ornithosis ("bird disease"),
since it is by no means
confined to parakeets and
parrots, as used to be thought,

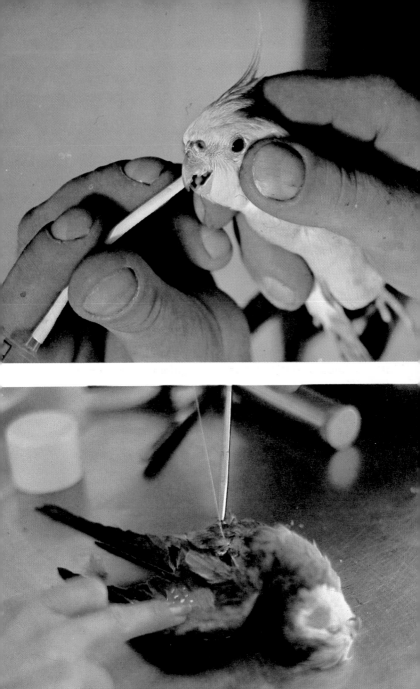

A Lutino Cockatie

but affects other kinds of birds as well. This all-too-familiar disease can also be transmitted to man; in the past it has frequently resulted in the patient's death. To aid in the control of psittacosis, [in Germany] every aviculturist dealing with parakeets and parrots has to keep a record of birds added to or leaving his stock. In accordance with the psittacosis law, he also has to pass a test, as already described in the chapter on breeding.

The disease occurs predominantly among uncontrolled large populations of parakeets, where imports and constant buying and selling are an added risk factor. On the other hand, infection from wild birds can never be entirely ruled out.

In man, psittacosis manifests itself as a flu-like illness. For this reason, every responsible aviculturist or fancier who observes an increasing number of mortalities of unknown cause among the birds in his care should initiate an examination of fecal specimens or of the dead birds themselves. These investigations and any further measures that may be necessary are carried out by the veterinary officer of the relevant local authority. If one prefers, one can have the analyses carried out privately, at one's own expense, by various private institutes or universities, but if the result is positive one still has to notify the authorities. Fortunately, psittacosis has since become curable, both in animals and humans, by means of antibiotics, and it is no longer necessary (as it used to be) to destroy the entire collection of birds.

It is not possible in a book of this scope to deal with any other bird diseases in detail. I would, therefore, advise the interested reader to consult Heinz-Sigurd Raethel's book *Bird Diseases*. There, a whole range of diseases receives detailed attention, as do their causes and prognosis. An accurate diagnosis is difficult for the layman in any case. I

would prefer to use the space available to me here to talk about preventive measures, so that from the outset the risk of disease can be kept to a minimum. To exclude it altogether is not possible, unfortunately.

At all times the most important prerequisite is cleanliness, both of the cage and aviary and the food. Regular cleaning of the cage bottom and aviary floor is imperative, as is thorough disinfecting at least twice a year. In a very dirty environment, mites, bacteria, and worms are given an excellent chance to proliferate, and they can do a great deal of harm to the birds. Birds infested with mites or lice should be treated with a commercial mite spray or powder—but the eyes, head, and beak must be protected. The whole aviary or cage should be treated at the same time to prevent the survival of any parasites in their hiding places.

Infestation with worms is becoming increasingly common in hobbyists' stocks. The worm eggs are transmitted via the excreta of free-living birds or infested new arrivals. Heavily infested birds grow so weak that they offer no resistance to the parasites at all when suffering from what would normally be described as a perfectly harmless cold; often this results in the bird's death. As a safeguard the birds are wormed twice a year, in the spring and fall. The anthelminthic is mixed into the drinking water or, alternatively, injected straight into the esophagus. Where the former method is chosen, the Cockatiels' drinking water is withheld for two days preceding the treatment, as are all foods (such as greenfood and fruit) with a high water content, to encourage the birds to take in the required amount. It is quite astonishing, sometimes, just how many dead worms one can find in the droppings after the treatment has been given.

Other diseases, e.g.,

inflammations of the stomach and intestine, can be prevented, particularly in a cage bird, by observing very carefully exactly what the Cockatiel ingests while it is free in the room. The chewing of house plants, newspapers, wall paper, leftover human food, or (worst of all) plastic bags can have devastating consequences, including death caused by suffocation.

As already mentioned, Cockatiels are extremely hardy birds and not particularly prone to disease. In captivity they have a life span of fifteen to twenty years.

The change of plumage which happens twice a year, the molt, is not a disease but an essential regeneration of the feathers. During this period a diet rich in vitamins is particularly important, as the birds' resistance is significantly lowered. Any commercial products which claim to stimulate the molt can, however, be ignored with a clear conscience. These are quite ineffective as a rule, and

where the birds receive a healthy and varied diet they are not needed in any case. As a result of frequent fluctuations in temperature or of drafts, an intermediate molt may occur; but if this runs a normal course and the cause is removed, it should give no grounds for concern.

Something that must be condemned as a serious vice is the pathological feather plucking which particularly occurs in larger parrots kept by themselves. Feather-pluckers pull out individual feathers, chew on the quill, and then pull out another, starting all over again, until completely bald patches appear. Not infrequently these patches become inflamed since growing replacement feathers are immediately pulled out again too. The cause of this pathological behavior has not yet been fully explained. So far, good results have been achieved by administering sodium chloride in solution and providing fruit-tree branches for the birds to chew.

A Pearl Pied Cockatie[l]

A tame Cockatiel flying free in the room all too easily sustains a broken wing or leg as a result of flying into a pane of glass or some other obstacle which it could not recognize in time. No attempts at first aid (such as applying a splint, etc.) should be made by the layman. It is vital to obtain veterinary help as quickly as possible.

In the case of excessively long claws or too long an upper or lower mandible, however, one can deal with it oneself. Claws are trimmed with the nail scissors pointing downwards. Care must be taken not to injure the blood vessel that extends into the claw, as this can result in inflammations. The blood vessel is clearly visible when the foot is held against the light. The mandible is carefully filed down with a nail file. For this, the bird's head is held between the thumb and index finger so that the bird cannot bite with his powerful beak. To keep the beak open during treatment, a small twig or similar object may be inserted between the upper and lower mandible; the bird will then bite firmly on it. To prevent injuries (such as tears and cracks), the mandible is rubbed with cooking oil prior to being filed.

Preening occupies much of a Cockatiel's time.

— *Varieties*

Like other bird species that are regarded as domesticated (e.g., the Budgerigar), the Cockatiel also has produced a number of mutations (color varieties). In circles of fanciers or at the bigger shows one encounters not only the wild-colored (gray) Cockatiels but also white, yellow, pied, pearled, bordered, cream, and cinnamon varieties. The various mutations have evolved sporadically, some of them in different localities at the same time, due to a sudden change in the genetic material. By means of careful selective breeding, notably backcrossing (inbreeding), it was possible to stabilize the abnormal color varieties and improve them both in respect to size and type. Deviations in the color of the plumage of some birds also occur in the wild, but there they quickly disappear again as a result of natural selection. Because the birds are more conspicuous, they readily fall prey to their enemies.

For the fancier of color varieties the rich color range of the Cockatiels offers a vast and interesting field of activity, and some breeder or other may well get a chance to raise a new color variety in his aviaries. A prerequisite for the breeding of mutations is, however, at least a basic knowledge of general genetics and its laws, otherwise there will inevitably be disappointments. I would also advise every breeder of mutations to keep an accurate breeding record which contains the pedigree of all breeding birds and their descendants. A conscientiously kept breeding record (either a book or a card system) makes it easy later on to select suitable birds from among the descendants for further breeding in order to attain the desired goal.

Basic Genetics

If we wish to breed Cockatiels, a basic knowledge of genetics is essential. All organisms consist of cells. Inside the cell nucleus lie the chromosomes with the units of heredity (genes), which are arranged somewhat like strings of beads. In cells of the body each chromosome is present in duplicate; that is, each cell has a double (diploid) set of chromosomes. If every gene is identified by a letter, then the wild color, gray, would be described as *GG*. In the gametes (egg and sperm cells) the chromosome pairs are separated and distributed into two cells. During fertilization the male and female gamete each contribute a single (haploid) set of chromosomes so that the fertilized cell and all its descendants (which result from division) again have a diploid set of chromosomes. In the case of the color varieties, the gene for "wild gray" is replaced by, say, the gene for white. The inheritance of these color variations is usually recessive to the dominant wild color; that is, they do not manifest themselves (they do not appear in the phenotype).

Gregor Mendel was the first to discover certain genetic laws. Let us look at an example: In the parental (P) generation, we mate a homozygous (*GG*, since dominant) wild-colored Cockatiel with a homozygous (*gg*, since recessive) white hen. The descendants—also known as the F_1 (first filial) generation—all look identical, i.e., gray like the dominant father. Mendel's First Law: If two homozygous races are crossed with each other, then all the descendants in the F_1 generation are identical to each other. This F_1 generation is, however, not homozygous like the parents but heterozygous (split). In other words, the young birds receive the gene *G* from the father and the gene *g* from the mother, which means they are of the genotype *Gg*. In the phenotype, however, the gene for white is masked by the gene for gray.

Mendel's Second Law: If the F_1 generation are mated with each other, then the descendants in the F_2 (second filial) generation are not

A Silver Cockatie

**Figure I. Mendel's First Law:
The Law of Uniformity.**

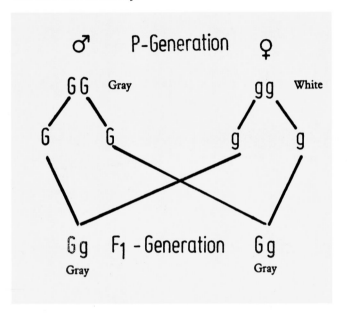

Geneticists and other scientists use the symbol ♂ (based on an old astrological sign for Mars) to represent the male sex, while ♀ (based on an old astrological sign for Venus) represents the female sex. The term homozygous indicates the presence of identical genes for a character, while heterozygous (split) indicates the presence of differing genes. Thus in the shorthand of genetics GG indicates a homozygous condition with two dominant gray genes, while Gg indicates a heterozygous condition with both a dominant gray gene and a recessive white gene.

— *Varieties* —

**Figure II. Mendel's Second Law:
The Law of Segregation**

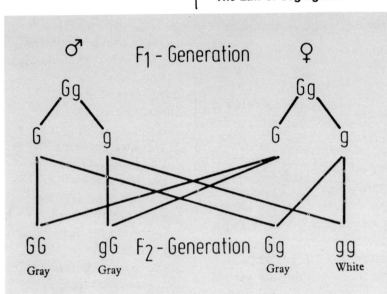

Figure III. Backcrossing of an F₁ bird with a homozygous parent.

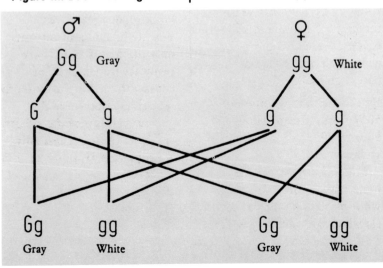

identical to each other but segregate in a certain ratio.

In the F_1 generation 50% of the gametes carry the gene G and 50% the gene g. This results in the F_2 generation in a phenotype of gray and white birds in the ratio of 3 : 1. In the genotype, on the other hand, the ratio is 1:2:1; i.e., 25% of the progeny are homozygous for gray, 50% are heterozygous, and 25% are homozygous for white. This means the desired color variation only reappears in the second generation and then in only 25% of the birds.

To increase the yield of white birds, we make use of the backcrossing method; that is, we mate a bird of the F_1 generation with a homozygous parent animal.

By this method we produce 50% grays split for white and 50% which are homozygous whites.

The following Cockatiel mutations are recessive to the wild-colored (gray) parakeets: (1) white with black eyes; (2) pied with black eyes; (3) pearled pied with black eyes; (4) silver-colored; (5) cream colored. What sex the birds are has no bearing on the inheritance of these characteristics. The percentages given have been calculated from hundreds of pairings and represent the average. It follows, therefore, that the breeder may well observe minor deviations when carrying out his own experiments. After backcrossing, for example, it is not uncommon for the first brood to consist only of heterozygous birds and the second brood only of homozygous recessives. For the breeding of mutants only pairings I and III are really favorable, as is, of course, the mating of purebred recessives, since here the genetic makeup of the progeny can be determined instantly. With pairing II, however, it is necessary to resort to control pairing.

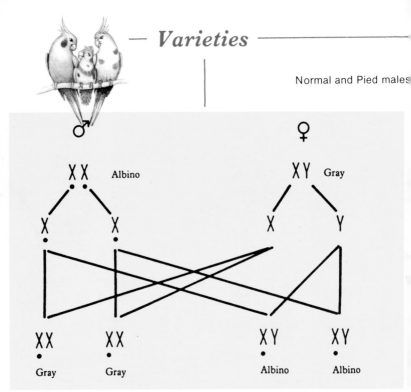

Figure IV. A basic sex-linked cross
of an albino male by a gray female.

Figure V. A sex-linked cross of a gray male
(homozygous) with an albino female.

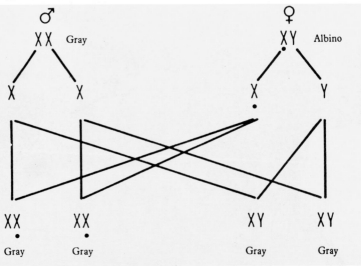

— *Varieties*

Sex-linked Inheritance

Besides the other chromosomes, each cell nucleus also contains two chromosomes which determine the sex of an individual. In birds, the males have two X chromosomes and the females one X and one Y chromosome each (exactly the reverse is the case in mammals). Therefore the Y chromosome is the one which determines the sex, since egg cells contain either an X or a Y chromosome. Thus the fertilized ovum contains either two X chromosomes (and a male will result) or an X and a Y chromosome (in which case we will get a female). Now there are a number of color varieties for which inheritance is sex-linked; i.e., the gene for the mutation is located on the X chromosome. Since hens have only a single X chromosome, they are always purebred. Cocks, on the other hand, may be heterozygous (when only one X chromosome carries the color mutation). In this case the wild color from the other X chromosome is masking the mutation.

Let us take a look at the different mating possibilities: If we mate an albino cock (xx) with a wild-colored hen (XY) the progeny will consist of albino females and gray males that are heterozygous (that is, one X chromosome will be carrying the variant color).

If, on the other hand, we mate a wild-colored cock and an albino female, then all the offspring will be gray; that is, the color variant is only carried in a masked form in the genotype of the cocks.

When a heterozygous cock is mated with a wild-colored hen the progeny are divided as follows: 50% of the cocks will be wild-colored purebreds while the other 50% will be heterozygous. Of the females, on the other hand, 50% will be wild-colored and 50% albinos.

Varieties

Figure VII represents the pairing of a male from the F_1 generation in figure V with its mother (backcrossing). As a result, here in the F_1 generation we obtain 50% males split for gray and 50% albino males; among the females 50% will be wild-colored and 50% albinos.

As becomes apparent from the diagrams, pairings IV and VII are to be preferred. Diagram VII also shows the result of crossing the progeny from the F_1 generation in figure IV with each other. Both pairings make it easy to determine the hereditary makeup of the young. With pairing V one does not get progeny of the desired color variety, so one is obliged to backcross a heterozygous male with its albino mother (diagram VII). Pairing VII is employed very frequently as it results in particularly hardy offspring. Apart from wild-colored hens and heterozygous cocks, one also obtains birds of both sexes in the desired color.

The following color varieties have a sex-linked inheritance: (1) albinos (white birds with red eyes); (2) lutinos (yellow birds with red eyes); (3) black-eyed pearled and bordered.

In addition to the modes of inheritance mentioned above, pied Cockatiels sometimes show the "partially dominant" inheritance. This is the only explanation why the first generation of wild-colored x pied so often includes "pied-headed" birds. These, compared to the predominantly gray appearance of wild-colored birds, show lighter patches on the head, neck, and wings. If two such individuals are paired to each other, their offspring can include some very attractive Pieds.

It goes without saying that the inheritance schemes outlined above can also be applied to pairings of recessive and sex-linked mutations with one another. Some combinations of mutations and the progeny one can expect from them are described below under the individual mutations.

Varieties

A Pearl hen. Pearled Cockatiels occur both as red-eyed and black-eyed mutations.

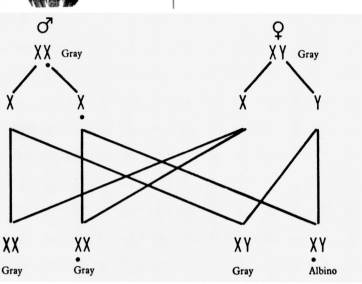

Figure VI. A sex-linked cross of a gray male (heterozygous) with a gray female.

Figure VII. A sex-linked cross of a gray male (heterozygous) with an albino female.

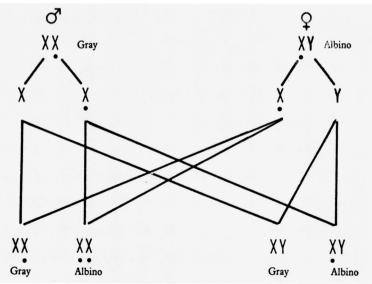

— *Varieties*

The Wild Color

By *wild-colored* the breeder of Cockatiel colors understands the normal, gray Cockatiels such as have already been described in the chapter on wild representatives of this species. For the breeding of mutations, wild-colored Cockatiels are required to improve type and size. The aviculturist should make sure that only the best stock is used for breeding purposes. As regards size, type, and posture, the *AZ* has set the following standards:

An elongated, slender appearance, made to look even slimmer than it is by the conical tail coming to a point. The erect posture should hold an angle of about sixty-five degrees and run in a beautifully straight line from the top of the head to the tip of the tail. The wings should lie close to the body and overlap the tail by about two fingers' breadth; they close without being crossed and cover the rump completely. From the beak, which does not project, the forehead extends to the crest in an even curve, while the crest curves outward in the opposite direction. There must be no feathers sticking out from the crest in the wrong direction, either opposite to or sideways from the even upward curve which terminates in the spurlike tip. That the crest be large and long is of particular importance. The total length of the bird should be 340 mm., whereby the 160 mm. length of the tail makes up nearly half the total length.

These standards apply to all the Cockatiel color variants as well. With regard to plumage color, the main points are that the colors are even and that the head is of a bright lemon yellow, with long yellow crest feathers and a round reddish orange patch on the cheeks.

Varieties —

White Cockatiels with Red Eyes (Albinos)

Albinos, generally regarded as the first Cockatiel mutation, made their debut in 1959, in the U.S.A. From there they reached the German Federal Republic in or around 1966, fetching fantastic prices (up to 8,000 DM per pair) during the first few years. However, because they were easy to propagate, they soon became less expensive, and today they cost little more than gray Cockatiels. The color of albino Cockatiels is not the pure white we are familiar with from other albino forms in the animal kingdom. The lemon-yellow head and red cheek patches have been preserved. The tail feathers, notably on the underside, are not white but a delicate yellow. The eyes are red, as they normally are in albino animals, and the feet are light gray. Cock and hen are identical in color, apart from the slightly more yellowish underside of the tail in the

hen. Regrettably, many albino Cockatiels have bald, unfeathered patches on the head, behind the crest. It is important to select only fully feathered breeders so that the baldness does not spread further. The inheritance of the factor for albinos is sex-linked. To achieve the best possible albinos from the point of view of size and type, it is better to breed with good-type gray birds than to pair albino with albino—otherwise, due to years of inbreeding, one can expect only fairly small descendants.

White Cockatiels with Black Eyes

Shortly after the first albinos had been bred came the white Cockatiels with black eyes. These birds are almost identical in appearance to the albinos. There are some distinguishing features, however: the eyes are black, and the white plumage seems brighter and purer because

In Bordered Cockatiels
spotting continues on
breast in diluted fo

there is less yellow in it. At
first, unfortunately, the white
Cockatiels with black eyes
were often crossed with true
albinos so that mixed varieties
resulted. Genetically, however,
the two mutations have
nothing in common. The
inheritance of white Cockatiels
with black eyes is recessive.
They have always had a
shadowy existence alongside
the albinos, partly because they
were never properly recognized, and they remain of only
minor significance to this day.

Yellow Cockatiels (Lutinos)

Yellow Cockatiels, also
referred to as lutinos, are by
no means bright yellow
parakeets similar to lutino
Budgerigars; they are albino
birds with a greater or lesser
tinge of yellow. This yellow
color variety also possesses red
eyes. The word *lutino* is
derived from the Latin and
means something like "yellow
lipochrome." In other words,
the lutinos are albinos with

lipochrome pigment. So far,
the yellow Cockatiel cannot be
regarded as a mutation in its
own right since a pairing of
yellow x yellow invariably
results in albinos again. Hence
the offers of such Cockatiels
advertised in the hobbyist
magazines are misleading, since
the lutinos are really nothing
more than albinos with a
plumage tending towards a
yellow color.

Pearled Cockatiels

The pearled Cockatiel
mutation was first bred abroad.
The ground color of the
plumage is of a somewhat
lighter shade, and there are
white to yellowish spots of
color on the upper side and the
wings. The underside also
shows such a dappled pattern,
but less prominently so. The
crest—no longer lemon-yellow
all over—is grayish yellow,
lemon-yellow only at the root.
Rump, tail feathers, and under-
tail coverts are yellow. The
yellow upper tail coverts are

black at the tip. Pearled
Cockatiels leave the nest box
with beautifully contrasting
spots. Unfortunately, however,
the intensive coloration fades
with increasing age, notably in
cocks. Nevertheless, the
pearled effect of the plumage is
passed on genetically. Pearled
Cockatiels occur both as red-
eyed and black-eyed mutations,
although the black-eyed variety
is by far the most common
one. The inheritance of the
factor for pearled is sex-linked.
Depending on the intensity of
color of the plumage, breeders
differentiate between golden
and silver pearled Cockatiels.

Bordered Cockatiels

Similar to the pearled are the
bordered Cockatiels. In this
mutation, however—again a
sex-linked one—the pearled
feathers in the plumage of back
and wings have a dark or light
margin. Every single feather of
these birds, whose coloring is
richly contrasting, should if
possible have a dark or light

edge and be light or dark in
the center. The disadvantage of
fading colors with increasing
age unfortunately applies to
this pretty mutation as well.

Pied Cockatiels

In 1959—at the same time as
the albino appeared, and again
in the U.S.A.—a strain of
almost clear pieds was bred.
Today pied varieties are
possible in the various colors.
Since a uniform standard is
impossible where the very
diversely and irregularly
colored pieds are concerned,
the *AZ* Standard describes the
color and markings of the ideal
pied Cockatiel as follows:
"There is no difference in size,
form, shape, and ground color
between cock and hen. The
pied markings should amount
to 50% and be as symmetrical
and clearly defined as
possible."
The most handsome birds
have lemon-yellow heads.
There is a range of piedness,
from lightly flecked pied-

headed birds, through all kinds of irregular distributions of body color, to almost white birds with a few gray feathers. The inheritance of this mutation is partially dominant, as already mentioned in the section on basic genetics. In order to obtain good pieds, one should mate the predominantly dark-colored young birds from the pairing pied x wild-color with each other.

Very popular nowadays are the combinations of pieds and bordered or pearled Cockatiels. The pairing of pied with pearled or bordered results in very colorful-looking birds, which show the pearled or bordered effect in the dark portions of their plumage. These markings are interrupted only by the white or yellowish areas of color.

Cinnamon (Isabel) Cockatiels

The cinnamon (isabel) Cockatiels, also known as silver-colored, are very attractive birds. Forehead and head, including the feathers of cheeks and chin, show a lemon-yellow color. The shafts of the crest feathers are brownish, becoming yellowish as they approach the tip. The ear patches are reddish orange. All the rest of the plumage, gray in the wild-colored Cockatiel, looks brownish. The tail feathers are dark brown. The cinnamon-colored wings show whitish yellow patches. Generally speaking, therefore, the cinnamon Cockatiel looks cinnamon-colored all over. Strong variations in the color of the plumage are very common, however, making some birds look more brownish, others more gray. The more grayish Cockatiels have a silver-colored, pale gray appearance; for this reason they are sometimes offered for sale as "silver Cockatiels."

The coloration of the cinnamon Cockatiels is the result of a total or partial absence of black in the

Lutino youngsters *(abov*
Outstretched wing of t
Pearl Cockatiel *(belov*

plumage, comparable to the cinnamon-colored wavelike markings of the cinnamon Budgerigars. The inheritance of this factor is said to be recessive. Very light-colored variations, which look almost whitish brown, are described as cream-colored.

Other Colors

The multitude of color varieties in the Cockatiel has by no means been exhausted, and a lot of surprises may yet be in store for the interested specialist breeder. There are already a number of additional color mutations and modifications (variations in color which are not inheritable) which are, however, still awaiting programmed breeding, research, and standardization.

At the *AZ* National Show in 1973, for example, an olive-green Cockatiel was exhibited. This bird was said to have derived from clear gray with a

high yellow content in the plumage. Black Cockatiels have also been offered, but these are likely to have been the result of modification rather than mutation, since it was not possible to breed black descendants from them. Similar modifications have already been observed in Budgerigars, Zebra Finches, and Bullfinches.

Certain specialist breeders keep offering Cockatiel color varieties under really fantastic names in the bigger animal magazines, but when looked at more closely, these usually turn out to be quite ordinary color variants of the kinds already described. There is no end in sight, so far, for the history of Cockatiel color varieties, and the future will show what riches may yet be found by the hobbyist.

— *Showing* —

Increasingly, each year the various local breeding clubs and local branches of the *AZ* organize exhibitions for birds bred by their members. In the early days these shows were dominated by Budgerigars, Canaries, woodland birds, and small exotic species. Today, however, at the bigger shows, notably the regional and national events of the *AZ*, there are large parakeets. Along with the African lovebirds (Agapornids), Cockatiels are particularly well represented because of their willingness to produce mutations and their wide distribution in hobbyist circles.

In order to enter the bigger exhibitions for large parakeets, where the birds are awarded points by approved judges in accordance with a system of points laid down by the *AZ*, it is necessary to become a member of the *AZ*. Only when the aviculturist is a member will he be able to closed-band the progeny with officially recognized breeder's bands.

These bands bear the name of the society (*AZ-AGZ*), the membership number of the breeder, the year the birds were bred, and a serial number.

Important, too, is the acquisition of a few regulation show cages. Their exact form, color, and dimensions are given in the *AZ* Standard published by the *AZ*. Because the show cages are rather small in relation to the bird to be exhibited (external dimensions 465 x 245 x 400 mm.), the prospective inhabitant needs to become accustomed to the narrow space over a longish period of time. In this way one obviates the possibility that the bird may damage its plumage or cause itself some other injury during the exhibition, which after all (from the time the bird arrives) may amount to as much as three or four days. Furthermore, it is essential that the bird be in good condition for the show. How else would the judge be able to make a fair decision?

Showing

Training the bird for exhibition should begin very early in its life. One starts off by leaving it in the show cage for a short period and then for increasingly longer spells. To adapt it to show conditions, one uses a wooden or judge's stick and lets several strangers walk past the cage. The young Cockatiel gets used to the confining cage more quickly if he is offered special tidbits (such as millet sprays) inside it. A good show training guarantees that the bird, at real exhibitions later on, will perch properly and present himself at his best. A bird that is nervous and anxious all the time, constantly running around on the bottom of the cage or hanging onto the wire by its claws and damaging its plumage in the process, has to be disqualified.

Only birds in good condition whose colors and markings are fully developed can be admitted to the show. This excludes emaciated or obese animals or birds that have recently raised young or are just beginning to molt.

The birds brought in for the show are classed into different breed and color categories and then judged by various criteria such as condition, size, type, carriage, etc. From the best of each class the judges subsequently pick the best of the group. If two birds score the same number of points, the younger bird is given preference over the older one, and the hen is given preference over the cock. To ensure a fair judgment, the *AZ* has issued the following guidelines by which the breeder can get a rough idea before the show as to how many points his birds are likely to score.

Condition	20 points
Size	15 points
Type, posture, wing position	20 points
Feet, toes, claws	10 points
Color and markings	35 points
	100 points

— *Showing* —

Children can have fun tami[
their Cockatie[

The following scores and evaluations may be attained:

90-100 pts.	Excellent	Gold Medal
85-89 pts.	Very Good	Silver Medal
80-84 pts.	Good	Bronze Medal
75-79 pts.	Satisfactory	

In accordance with the Standard for Large Parakeets, Cockatiels are exhibited in Group III. The different color varieties are arranged into the following classes:

Class Code Number

Group/Class	Breeder	Adv
III/1 Wild-colored	63	113
III/2 White/Yellow	64	114
III/3 Pearled/Bordered	65	115
III/4 Pied	66	116
III/5 Cinnamon (Isabel)	67	117
III/6 Other Mutations	68	118

In addition, birds that have been purchased may be exhibited in the Open Class ("Class X"). The winner of this class competes with the other group winners for Best Parakeet in Show.

What exactly is the purpose of an exhibition? A bird show enables the breeder to compare his own birds with those raised by other aviculturists. The goal of every breeder should be to get as close to the ideal bird (as prescribed by the Standard) as he possibly can. To try and achieve this, only birds close to this ideal should be chosen for pairing. Breeding, after all, not only means propagation but also selection. If the aviculturist practices such selective breeding, he can compare his results with those of other breeders, have his birds evaluated by a neutral judge, and thus be kept aware of how he is progressing and where improvements need to be made. For this reason, exhibiting is of enormous benefit and importance, particularly where breeders of color varieties are concerned. Everybody has to learn, and one should never lose hope if he does not succeed instantly in producing the best bird in the show. Just to take part is of tremendous value. One may not do well the first time, but one can still learn a lot by being there. As I said: breeding does not merely mean

propagating; it also means selecting the best.

Further hints and advice on showing your birds can be obtained from experienced breeders and exhibitors belonging to the various local societies, through regular attendance at shows, and by studying the specialist literature, notably the society periodicals and the Standard. These always contain discussions of the news and problems concerned with breeding, keeping, and exhibiting.

Bibliography

The following books, also published by T.F.H. Publications, Inc., are recommended for further reading.

Allen, Gerald R. and Allen, Connie. 1981 *Cockatiel Handbook.*

Enehjelm, C. af. 1981. *Cages and Aviaries.*

Forshaw, Joseph M. 1977. *Parrots of the World.*

Moon, Mrs. E. L. 1976. *Experiences with My Cockatiels.*

Raethel, H. S. 1981. *Bird Diseases.*

Smith, George A. 1978. *Encyclopedia of Cockatiels.*

Sturman, Julie, with Schults, Dorothy. 1980. *Breeding Cockatiels.*

Tartak, Laura M. 1979. *Cockatiels.*

Teitler, Risa. 1979. *Taming and Training Cockatiels.*

Index —

93

KW-150

THE ABC'S OF
COCKATIELS